modern readers — stage 2

Johnny's First Kiss

João de Magalhães

Richmond

© JOÃO DE MAGALHÃES, 2005

Richmond

Diretoria: *Paul Berry*
Gerência editorial: *Sandra Possas*
Coordenação de revisão: *Estevam Vieira Lédo Jr.*
Coordenação de produção gráfica: *André Monteiro, Maria de Lourdes Rodrigues*
Coordenação de produção industrial: *Wilson Troque*

Projeto editorial: *Kylie Mackin*

Edição e preparação de texto: *Kylie Mackin*
Assistência editorial: *Gabriela Peixoto Vilanova*
Revisão: *Fernanda Marcelino*
Projeto gráfico de miolo e capa: *Ricardo Van Steen Comunicações e Propaganda Ltda./Oliver Fuchs*
Edição de arte: *Christiane Borin*
Ilustrações de miolo e capa: *Attílio*
Diagramação: *Formato Comunicação*
Pré-impressão: *Helio P. de Souza Filho, Marcio H. Kamoto*
Impressão e acabamento: *BMF Gráfica e Editora*
Lote: 266604

Dados Internacionais de Catalogação na Publicação (CIP)
(Câmara Brasileira do Livro, SP, Brasil)

Magalhães, João de
　　Johnny's first kiss / João de Magalhães. —
São Paulo : Moderna, 2004. — (Modern readers ; stage 2)

　　1. Inglês (Ensino fundamental) I. Título.
II. Série.

04-0910   CDD-372.652

Índices para catálogo sistemático:
1. Inglês : Ensino fundamental   372.652

ISBN 85-16-04094-1

Reprodução proibida. Art. 184 do Código Penal e Lei 9.610 de 19 de fevereiro de 1998.

Todos os direitos reservados.

RICHMOND
EDITORA MODERNA LTDA.
Rua Padre Adelino, 758 — Belenzinho
São Paulo — SP — Brasil — CEP 03303-904
Central de atendimento ao usuário: 0800 771 8181
www.richmond.com.br
2018

Impresso no Brasil

A New School

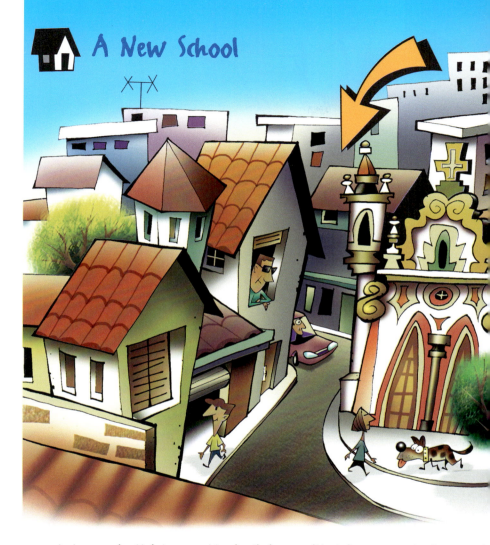

Johnny is thirteen. He is living with his **parents** in a new **neighborhood**. It's his first day at a new school. But Johnny is not very happy. He doesn't know the other kids there.

It's early in the morning. **Outside** the sun is **shining**. Johnny and his mother are talking in the kitchen.

Johnny – But I want to stay with my best friends Tom, Chris, and Bobby! What about **soccer practice**, Mom? I'm on the **team**. Don't you remember?

Mom – Of course I do. But you'll make new friends at your new school, Johnny.

Johnny – But I don't want to be the **'new kid'** that **everyone** talks about. It's terrible when other kids **make fun of you**.

Mom – I know it's difficult to **change** schools, Johnny. And It's **hard** to **leave** good friends. But **trust** me! After a week, you won't be the new kid anymore!

Johnny – Come on, Mom! **Stop kidding!** If I don't like the new school, I'm not going to stay there. I'm going back to my old school.

Two Months Later...

It's **lunchtime.** Johnny is at home. He is **in a hurry** because he is going out with his friends from his new school. He runs **down the stairs.** His mother is preparing **lunch.**

Johnny – Bye Mom! I'm going to play **soccer** with my friends!

Mom – Hey! Lunch is **almost ready**! Don't you want to eat?

Johnny – No thanks Mom. I'm late! I'll eat something later!

Johnny's new **school friends** are Nick, Lou and Fred. They are **classmates**. They play soccer on the school **team** and do lots of things together. They call **themselves** "The **Gang**".

Cynthia is Johnny's classmate too. When he is not with The Gang, he likes to **spend** time with her. Johnny and Cynthia usually study together. After school, they always **chat** on the phone.

It's 10 o'clock in the morning. It's break time and the kids are chatting in the school yard.

Nick – Hey, Johnny! Come with us to Fred's house after school!

Johnny – I can't. Cynthia and I are going to study together for the exam tomorrow. My mom is going to help us.

Nick – Come on, Johnny! Fred's parents are **out of town**. It's going to be **fun**!

Fred – Yes! Come with us, Johnny!

Johnny – All right, I'll go! But first, I need to call my mom and Cynthia!

Making fun of Johnny

At Fred's house, the kids are **laughing** and **telling jokes.** They are eating **junk food** and drinking **soda**. Johnny **forgets** to call his mother and Cynthia. Later the telephone **rings**. Tony, Fred's older brother, answers the phone.

"Hello, this is Tony speaking. Who is this? Johnny's mom... OK, **hold on!**"

Tony – Hey, Johnny, it's your **mommy** on the phone! Ha, ha, ha!

Johnny answers the phone.

"Hi Mom…"

"Johnny, your friend Cynthia is looking for you **everywhere**," his mother says. "What are you doing at Fred's house? Don't you have an exam tomorrow?"

Johnny is **embarrassed**. "Sorry Mom! I'll call Cynthia. And I'll study later on, OK? Bye."

Johnny hangs up the phone. He turns to his friends.

Johnny – Well, I think my mom is **mad** at me.

Nick – Hey, Johnny, don't worry. All moms are the **same**. It's **no big deal**!

Johnny – **Anyway**, it's late. I need to go! Bye **guys**!

Tony starts to **make fun** of Johnny.

"Mommy, Mommy, Sorry! Hey, and don't forget to call CYNTHIA! Ha, ha, ha!"

Johnny - Shut up, Tony!
Fred and Nick – See you, Johnny!
Later at night, Johnny arrives home. He tells his mother he is going to study the **next** morning before school. He calls Cynthia and **apologizes** to her. They talk on the phone for a long time.

Bad Grades, Bad News

The **following** morning, Johnny is **still** sleeping. His mother enters his bedroom. She is very **upset**.

Mom – **Wake up,** Johnny! Wake up!
Johnny – Oh, Mom... What time is it?
Mom – It's 7:45 and you're late for school! **Hurry up** and **get ready**! You don't have time for breakfast! And **by the way,** I want to see your exam results later!

Johnny gets a bad **grade** on the exam. Because of this, he doesn't want to go home immediately. He decides to go to Fred's house with the gang.

The kids play video games all afternoon. Tony has a **pack of cigarettes**. He takes one and passes the pack to Fred, Nick, and Lou. They all take a cigarette. Tony gives the pack to Johnny.

Johnny – No thanks, Tony. I don't smoke. **Actually**, I don't like cigarettes!

Fred – Why don't you **try**? It's **cool**!

Johnny tries to smoke and...
Johnny – Arghhhh! It's **awful**!
The boy feels horrible. He starts to **cough** and to **breathe** with difficulty. Fred makes fun of him.
Fred – You don't know how to smoke, Johnny!
All the kids laugh at Johnny.

One mistake after another

Next day at school, Johnny is talking to Cynthia when the boys **arrive**. He sees them and **feels** embarrassed.

Johnny – OK, so... I'll see you later Cynthia.
Cynthia – Johnny, are we going to study together this afternoon?
Johnny – Well, I'm not sure... I'll call you, OK?

Johnny leaves Cynthia. She is upset. "The Gang" asks Johnny if he is **dating** Cynthia.

Johnny – No, not **really**!
Lou – Good! Because we are going to have a party and Julia will be there. She's **crazy about** you.
Johnny – Really?
Nick – Yeah, Johnny. Everybody knows that!
Fred – Hey, Johnny, you're a **lucky** guy! Julia is the best-looking girl at school.

It's late in the evening. Johnny is at home. He is talking to Cynthia on the phone. She is still upset.

Johnny – Hi, Cynthia. I'm sorry about today. Let's study together tomorrow after class! We can meet at the library.

Cynthia – I don't think it's a good idea, Johnny. Every time your friends **appear**, you act strange around me.

Johnny – Sorry, Cynthia. It's because... Well, I **get** embarrassed!

Cynthia – No Johnny. I think you are **ashamed** of me. Listen, I have to go now. Talk to you later.

Some good advice

Johnny is in his room. He is **feeling down.** He really cares about Cynthia. Now, she is **disappointed** in him. Suddenly, someone **knocks** on his bedroom door. It's his father.

Dad – Johnny… can I come in?
Johnny – Sure Dad!
Dad – Johnny, your mother is a little worried about you. Is everything okay?

Johnny – Not really, Dad. I know Mom is disappointed in me, and now Cynthia is upset too...

Johnny's father sees that his son is **sad**. He sits down **next** to him.

Dad – Johnny, sometimes we do things we don't want to, just to **please** other people. Sometimes, we **hurt** people we like. Sometimes, we hurt **ourselves**.

Johnny – Thanks, Dad!

Johnny's dad **hugs** his son.

Planning the Party

After class, "the gang" **arranges** the last **details** of the party. Fred and Lou tell Johnny that Julia will be there. They are going to **meet** at Fred's house around 8:00 pm. **In the meantime,** Johnny tries to tell Cynthia about the party. But she is too **busy** to talk. Later, the kids go to soccer practice.

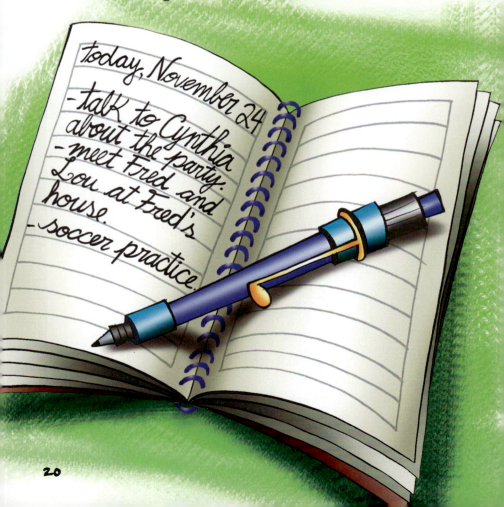

Johnny arrives home from soccer practice. He asks his mother if there are any messages for him. But there are **none**. He takes a shower and phones Cynthia. He wants to **invite** her to the party. Johnny is planning to tell her that he likes her. But Cynthia's **line** is always **busy**. It's almost 8 o'clock.

Johnny – Mom, I'm going to the party!

Mom – Do you want your father to **pick you up** later?

Johnny – No Mom, Nick's dad is going to give us a lift. Bye!

A party of surprises

It's **"party time"** at Fred's house. The kids are all **excited**. Julia is there with a group of girls. Music is playing and some kids are dancing. The boys are in one **corner** and the girls are in another. Julia **smiles** at Johnny. The boys **encourage** Johnny to go and talk to her.

Johnny – Hey, guys, listen. I'm not really interested in Julia...

Fred – Hey, Johnny, she's smiling at you. Now is your chance!

Lou – Yeah man! Go and talk to her! Do it for us! Do it for the gang!

Johnny doesn't want to let his friends down. **At the same time**, he is thinking about Cynthia. But he finally **agrees** to talk to Julia.

Johnny – Hi, Julia!

Julia – Oh, hello Johnny... Hey, the guys say you are the best player on the soccer team.

Johnny – Well, I guess I'm all right!

To Johnny's surprise, Julia puts her arms around him and kisses him. At this moment, Cynthia arrives at the party. She sees Johnny with Julia!

Fred and Lou are next to Cynthia. They decide to **tease** her.

Fred – Johnny is a really lucky guy!
Lou – Yes, he sure is!
Cynthia looks angrily at Fred and Lou. Then she turns and walks away.
Fred – Hey, Cynthia, where are you going? Don't you want to stay for the rest of the party?
Cynthia – You guys are really stupid, just like your friend, Johnny!

Doing the right thing

Cynthia **runs quickly out of** the house. Just then, Johnny sees her. He turns to Julia.

Johnny – Sorry Julia, but I have to talk to someone.

Johnny runs **across** the **living room.** His friends try to stop him, but he **pushes them away**. He wants to talk to Cynthia before she goes away.

Cynthia is **already** outside. She is crying.

Johnny – Cynthia! Hey, Cynthia! Wait a minute!
Cynthia – Johnny, why don't you go back inside? Your **girlfriend** is waiting for you.
Johnny – She's not my girlfriend. I don't care about her. I'm **hanging out** with the gang just to be cool.
Cynthia – I don't believe you, Johnny!
Johnny – Cynthia, I really care about you. The party is **over** for me too. Let me take you home.
Cynthia – No thanks. My father is coming to pick me up. Look, that's him now.

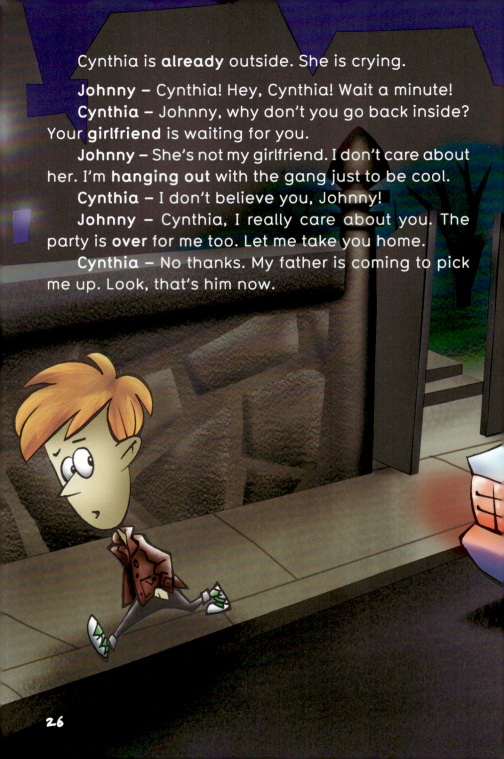

A car stops in front of the house. Johnny looks at Cynthia. For the first time, she sees that he is really **sad**.

As Johnny starts to walk away, he is thinking – "I'm really stupid. Now I know I really like Cynthia but she hates me."

Cynthia enters the car. Johnny is walking away when he hears a voice.

Cynthia – Hey, Johnny! We can take you home if you want.

Johnny turns round and sees Cynthia smiling at him.

Another school day is beginning. Johnny is having breakfast with his mother.

Mom – What time will you be home, Johnny?

Johnny – Well, Mom, after class I have soccer. Then I'm meeting Cynthia. We're doing a Geography project together.

Mom – Remember your first day at school? Now, look at you! You're not the "new kid" anymore, son.

Johnny – You're wrong, Mom. I AM a "new kid"!

He **grabs** his **backpack**, kisses his mother and goes to school.

KEY WORDS

The meaning of each word corresponds to its use in the context of the story (see page number, 00)

across (25) através
advice (18) conselho
agree, agrees (23) concordar
almost (6) quase
already (26) já
apologize, apologizes (11) desculpar-se
appear (17) aparecer
arrange, arranges (20) combinar
arrive, arrives (23) chegar
ashamed (17) envergonhado
awful (14) horrível
backpack (28) mochila
breathe (14) respirar
busy (20) ocupado
change (5) mudar
chat, chatting (7) bater papo
classmate (7) colega de sala
cool (13) legal, maneiro
corner (22) canto
cough (14) tossir
date, dating (16) sair com
detail (20) detalhe
disappointed (18) desapontada
embarrassed (10) sem graça
encourage (22) encorajar
everyone (4) todo mundo
everywhere (10) todo lugar
excited (22) animado

feel, feels (15) sentir
following (12) seguinte
forget, forgets (9) esquecer
fun (8) divertido
gang (7) turma
get, gets (17) ficar
girlfriend (26) namorada
grab, grabs (28) pegar
grade (13) nota
guys (10) caras
hard (5) difícil
hate, hates (27) odiar
hear, hears (27) escutar, ouvir
hug, hugs (19) abraçar
hurt (19) magoar, ferir
invite (21) convidar
knock, knocks (18) bater (na porta)
laugh, laughing (9) rir
leave, leaves (5) deixar, partir
line (21) linha telefônica
living room (25) sala de estar
lucky (16) sortudo
lunch, lunchtime (6) almoço, hora do almoço
mad (10) brava, com raiva
meet, meeting (20) encontrar
mistake (15) erro
mommy (9) mamãezinha
neighborhood (3) vizinhança
next (11) próximo

none (21) nenhum
ourselves (19) nós mesmos
outside (3) lado de fora
over (26) terminado, acabado
parents (3) pais, pai e mãe.
plan, planning (20) planejar
please (19) satisfazer
news (12) notícias
quickly (25) rapidamente
ready (6) pronto
really (16) de verdade, sério
ring, rings (9) tocar
sad (19) triste
school friends (7) colegas de escola
shine, shining (3) brilhar
smile, smiles (22) sorrir
soccer (4) futebol
soda (9) refrigerante
spend (7) gastar
still (12) ainda
team (4) time, equipe
tease (24) provocar
trust (5) confiar
themselves (7) eles mesmos
try, tries (13) tentar
upset (12) chateado

Expressions
Actually (13) na verdade, na realidade.
Anyway (10) De qualquer maneira
at the same time (23) ao mesmo tempo
by the way... (12) a propósito...
crazy about (16) louco por, gostar muito de
down the stairs (6) escada abaixo
feel down, feeling down (18) sentir-se triste, sentindo-se triste
get ready! (12) apronte-se!
hanging out with (26) andar com, andar na companhia de
hold on! (9) espere um pouco!
Hurry up! (12) Apresse-se!
in a hurry (6) com pressa
In the meantime... (20) Enquanto isso...
junk food (9) comida não muito saudável
make fun of someone (4) gozar alguém, fazer chacota
new kid (4) novo garoto (da escola, da vizinhança)
no big deal (10) sem problemas, nada demais
out of town (8) fora da cidade
pack of cigarettes (13) maço de cigarros
party time (22) hora de festa
pick someone up (21) pegar alguém, buscar
push away, pushes away (25) empurrar, tirar do caminho
run out of (25) correr para fora
Shut up! (11) Cale-se!
soccer practice (4) treino de futebol
Stop kidding! (5) Pare de brincar!
telling jokes (9) contando piadas
Wake up! (12) Acorde!

ACTIVITIES

Before Reading

1. Read the title and look at the picture on the cover. What kind of story do you think this is?

While Reading
A New School

2. Johnny is thirteen and he doesn't want to go to the new school. Why?

At School

3. Now Johnny has some new school friends. What are their names?
4. Who is the friend Johnny always chats to on the phone?

Making fun of Johnny

5. Check (✓) what sort of things the kids do at Fred's house.
    - ( ) Play video games.
    - ( ) Watch movies.
    - ( ) Eat junk food.
    - ( ) Read stories.
    - ( ) Tell jokes.
    - ( ) Make phone calls.
    - ( ) Laugh a lot.

6. Someone calls Johnny on the phone at Fred's house. Who is it and why?

Bad Grades, Bad News

7. Put these events in order (1 – 5):
    - a. ( ) Johnny tries to smoke a cigarette.
    - b. ( ) It's 7:45 and Johnny is late for school.
    - c. ( ) Johnny receives a bad grade on the exam.
    - d. ( ) Johnny's mom wakes him up.
    - e. ( ) Johnny goes to Fred's house.

One mistake after another

8. At school, Cynthia is upset with Johnny. What is the reason?

Some good advice

9. Who is disappointed in Johnny?

10. Who gives Johnny some good advice?

Planning the party

11. Johnny does many things before the party. Write them in the correct order:
    a. ( ) phones Cynthia.
    b. ( ) goes to soccer practice.
    c. ( ) takes a shower.
    d. ( ) arranges the last details of the party.

A party of surprises

12. Julia kisses Johnny.
    a. Do you think she really likes him?
    b. Does he like her?

13. What happens when Cynthia arrives at the party?

Doing the right thing

14. At the end of the story, Johnny tells his mother that he is a 'New Kid'? What does he mean by this?

After Reading (Optional Activities)

15. Mini-Project:

    Imagine you are a journalist. Interview your classmates to find out how many of them come from a different place (e.g. neighborhood, town, city, state or country). Ask about the habits, climate, accent, culture, location etc., of the place. Ask them about their old schools.